Death and
on the Nile

A MURDER A LA CARTE MYSTERY PLAY

by

Peter De Pietro

SAMUEL
FRENCH

FOUNDED 1830

New York Hollywood London Toronto
SAMUELFRENCH.COM

ISBN **978-0-573-69598-8**   Printed in U.S.A.   #6197

IMPORTANT BILLING AND CREDIT REQUIREMENTS

All producers *of DEATH AND DECEIT ON THE NILE must* give credit to the Author of the Play in all programs distributed in connection with performances of the Play, and in all instances in which the title of the Play appears for the purposes of advertising, publicizing or otherwise exploiting the Play and /or a production. The name of the Author *must* appear on a separate line on which no other name appears, immediately following the title and *must* appear in size of type not less than fifty percent of the size of the title type.

DEATH AND DECEIT ON THE NILE

was first produced in 1992 aboard chartered cruises
on the Nile River in Egypt,from Luxor to Aswan,
and subsequently throughout the United States.
The original cast was as follows:

CAST (In Order of Appearance)

PROFESSOR DILLON DOBSON, PhD............ R.M. Himes
PERSON IN TRENCH COAT ....Richie Ridge
BENJAMIN PETERS ....Al Mohrmann
PRINCESS TARA OF MUNCHOVNIA ...Annie Fitzpatrick
JOE AL-ABDUL DI MICI ....Michael Kostroff
ESMIRELDA WHITE ....Susan Tabor
ZELDA LAVISH ....Richie Ridge
MICHAEL PETERS... Al Mohrmann

CAST OF CHARACTERS
(In Order of Appearance)

PROFESSOR DILLON DOBSON, Phd................................
Internationally renowned archeologist and expert on Egyptian history. He has invited the guests to cruise down the Nile to view his newest discovery--a treasure of immense bounty which he describes as the "Eighth Wonder of the World." 45-60 years.

PERSON IN TRENCH COAT...
Clothed in a trench coat, black fedora and a ski mask, s/he mysteriously lurks about. (Same actor as Zelda Lavish.)

BENJAMIN PETERS...
Astute writer who is writing a book on the recent discovery of artifacts in the Middle East and Egypt. Intelligent, dapper and authoritative. 35-40 years.

PRINCESS TARA OF MUNCHOVNIA..................................
Elegant princess of a small Eastern European country. A jet-setter, who dresses to the nines, boasts of the largest collection of jewels in Europe and wants the professor's find to add to her collection. 30 years.

JOE AL-ABDUL DIMICI...
Part Italian, part Egyptian and 100% greedy. A successful entrepreneur who is currently courting Princess Tara. A former lounge singer. 35-40 years.

ESMIRELDA WHITE...

Loveable, annoying, funny and daffy housekeeper to the professor. She is of English cockney heritage and still strong with accent. 40-50 years.

ZELDA LAVISH...

A strangely glamorous and exotic woman who claims to be a world-famous art dealer and a dear friend of James Bond. She is desperate to get her hands on the professor's find. Played by a man in a dress. 30-35 years.

MICHAEL PETERS..

Benjamin's twin brother. A hard-nosed detective. More outgoing, less intellectual than his brother. (Same actor as Benjamin). 35-40 years.

DEATH AND DECEIT ON THE NILE

Scene 1

(PROF. DILLON DOBSON, BENJAMIN PETERS and ESMIRELDA WHITE work the crowd. PROF. welcomes the guests and informs them they will soon be boarding the "Nile Princess". He congratulates them on being the first group of Westerners, aside from himself and his archeological team, who will set eyes on his recent discovery of ancient Egyptian jewels and treasure, which he has named "The Eighth Wonder of the World." ESMIRELDA dotes on the PROF., tells far-fetched stories of the treasure's discovery, which the Prof. corrects, and jokes with the guests. BENJAMIN casts doubt on the authenticity of the Professor's find. PERSON IN TRENCHCOAT lurks about.)

(All guests receive a Murder A La Carte dossier, which includes the limerick clues—scrambled so the guest must unscramble—a piece of Bribe Money, a Resolution Form and Murder A La Carte's Rules of the Game. A Murder A La Carte Production Manual is avaiable for rental from Samuel French, Inc. to instruct in the making of the dossiers.)

(When cued, PROF. takes front and center, MUSIC out. MAN IN TRENCHCOAT exits.)

PROF. Ladies and gentlemen, your attention please. Welcome. I want to thank you all for accepting my invitation to this mystifying and ancient land, Egypt. The desert sands outside appear dark and foreboding, but piercing through the dark ness are the bright beams of the moon. They are a beacon, which will lead us up the Nile, as they did the powerful Pharaohs of Kingdoms past. Soon we'll be boarding the "Nile Princess" and sailing to Aswan, where the most impressive archeological find of this century awaits us. It is the priceless treasure of King Pharclas (pronounced Fár-klus), who ruled supreme over the Egyptian "Middle Kingdom". I discovered the treasure just weeks ago. It dates from the 10th Century B.C., and is of such immense bounty and beauty, I have named it *(Big.)* the "Eighth Wonder of the World". And you, my friends, will be the first Westerners, aside from myself and my crew, ever to lay eyes on it.

BENJAMIN. Excuse me, Professor. What is the exact location of the treasure?

PROF. We uncovered it in the heart of the city of Aswan.

BENJAMIN. I find that unlikely, since Aswan has never been the site of excavated antiquities of value.

PROF. That is why my discovery is an archeological coup.

BENJAMIN. Is it a coup or a sham?

PROF. What are you saying?

BENJAMIN. The only significant ruins ever to be found in the vicinity of Aswan have been on Elephantine Island, which sits west of the city in the middle of the Nile, and compared to other discoveries in the Nile Valley, even those are paltry.

PROF. Listen, if you don't want to be a part of this exciting trip to an ancient bounty, I suggest you leave.

BENJAMIN. Oh, you're wrong. I so want to be a part of this... *(Changes tone.)* fabricated trip to nothing. *(Strong.)* I want to be the one who exposes you as the fake that you are.

(PRINCESS TARA storms in. She speaks with a thick Eastern European accent.)

TARA. Where is it? Where is treasure? I want treasure!

PROF. Ma'am, we all want a look at the treasure. Now, I was just explaining the trip, so please...

TARA. I do not want to look at treasure. I want to buy treasure.

PROF. You can buy a plastic replica of the treasure at one of the gift shops in Aswan.

TARA. *(Evil.)* You are patronizing me.

PROF. I just want to continue with my lecture.

TARA. Do you not know who I am? *(Livid.)* I am Princess Tara of Munchovnia!

PROF. Yeah, and I'm King Tut. Sit down.

TARA. I will call in Munchovnian Army. They will secure treasure for me.

PROF. *(Referring to her low-cut dress.)* Tell them to bring a sweater. You're going to catch a mighty chest cold.

TARA. You are evil man.

PROF. And you are an univited guest.

TARA. I want treasure.

PROF. Sit down.

TARA. You're not going to get away with this. You hear me?...

(JOE AL-ABDUL DIMICI enters in a zoot suit and a fez atop his head.)

TARA/JOE. You're not going to...

JOE. Get away from me, Princess. *(Spots TARA.)* Baby, Baby... Hey, you're not playing fair.

TARA. The game is over.

JOE. The game isn't over until I abduct you and make you my concubine.

TARA. I don't want to play anymore.

JOE. But "Bury the Treasure" is your favorite.
TARA. No.

(JOE pulls out a glittering necklace and dangles it.)

JOE. How about a little incentive?
PROF. *(With urgency.)* Where did you get that necklace?
JOE. It's a secret.
PROF. *(Takes necklace.)* The stones are cut exactly as those in the treasure of King Pharclas.
JOE. *(Pulls out another string of jewels.)* What about these?
PROF. Those too.
JOE. *(Pulls out yet another necklace.)* And these?
PROF. Yes. *(With revelation.)* You have been to the treasure!
JOE. No. I've been to K-Mart. These are paste. We use them in our game.
PROF. Sir, you have not been invited here. What is your name?
JOE. I am Joe Al-Abdul Dimici. Mom came from Cairo. Dad from Sicily. I'm from the good ole U. S. of A... Las Vegas to be exact. Do you know it?
PROF. The capitalistic oasis in the Nevada desert.
JOE. That's one way to look at it. I see it as America's temple of fun, fun, fun.
BENJAMIN. *(Sarcastic.)* You detect genuine treasure, Professor. Some "Eighth Wonder of the World"!
PROF. You cynics will be proven wrong. You wait and see. I'll get you. You hear me?...

(ESMIRELDA WHITE enters waving a butterfly net.)

PROF./ESMIRELDA. I'll get you...

ESMIRELDA. You writhing, fluttering thing you.

PROF. Mrs.. White, what are you doing?

ESMIRELDA. I'm trackin' down this rare butterfly, the
_____U.S.(Fill in venue.)_____U.S. (Fill in city.)

PROF. You were asked to remain outside during this welcoming reception.

ESMIRELDA. Oh yeah, you're right. I was. Sorry 'bout that, sir... Your Majesty... Your Royal Pain in the Dust Bin.

PROF. Mrs. White!

ESMIRELDA. Oh, don't go gettin' your ruffles all wrinkled.

PROF. Mrs. White you're dismissed!

ESMIRELDA. You don't want to dismiss me, *Sir.* I know too much. Remember?

PROF. Off with you.

ESMIRELDA. You'll have to drag me through the streets like St. Joan to get me on that boat. There's danger on that boat!

PROF. Off with you, you old battle-ax. Off, I say.

(PROFESSOR begins to drag ESMIRELDA out.)

ESMIRELDA. Be warned. All of ye. Dangeeer. There's nasty happenin's aboard that boat.

(ESMIRELDA lets out a curdling scream as they exit.)

JOE. Princess baby, you hear that? Nasty happenin's aboard that boat. I want a first-class cabin.

TARA. Yes. We go. I must get treasure to add to my family jewels.

JOE. *(Referring to her cleavage.)* Baby, your family jewels are fine just the way they are. Come on. Time for some fun, fun, fun.

(JOE and TARA exit. BENJAMIN takes front and center.)

BENJAMIN. Ladies and gentlemen, it is doubtful that you're going to see anything of value on this trip, so I would advise all of you to get a refund for the boat trip, and take in the sights of the mainland. *(PERSON IN TRENCHCOAT noticeably lurks about, walking in front of BENJAMIN, as he speaks.)* Cairo is a city which boasts of may fine museums-- museums which house the most extensive collection of Pharaonic treasures in the world. You may be wondering how I know so much about this mystifying land and the antiquities that are testament to it's monumental history. *(MAN IN TRENCHCOAT exits.)* My name is Benjamin Peters. I am an historian and a writer. I specialize in Middle Eastern and Egyptian cultures of long ago. *(Emphasizes the rhyme.)* The past, I decree, is the key to destiny. That little rhyme summarizes my philosophy. What we are today, is a direct result of what we were yesterday. Cause and effect. What we are now will shape what we will be tomorrow. *(With verve.)* Just as the ancient kings of Egypt did: aspire to high art and literature and in the future you'll be well-off. *(Gunshots ring out, hitting BENJAMIN.)* You'll be okay. *(Gunshots again.)* No you won't.

(BENJAMIN falls. ALL run in, except MAN IN TRENCHCOAT.)

TARA. Danger Dangeer!

PROF. What is happening? Oh my goodness, what is happening?

ESMIRELDA. Someone dial 411, dial 411.

JOE. That's 911.

TARA. Quiet, everybody, he's breathing. He's trying to say something.

BENJAMIN. *(Breathy.)* Beware the guise.

(BENJAMIN dies. TARA picks up his arm and drops it.)

TARA. He's dead.

PROF. What did he say?

TARA. He said...

BENJAMIN. *(Sits up, in full voice.)* Beware the guise!

(BENJAMIN dies.)

ESMIRELDA. Which guys? You guys?

(PROFESSOR addresses audience.)

PROF. Ladies and gentlemen, such a tragic hand of cards the ancient gods of Egypt have dealt us.

ESMIRELDA. That weren't from no ancient god. Those wounds came from a gun.

PROF. Mrs. White, I was just trying to be poetic.

ESMIRELDA. Stop bein' poetic and be helpful. Call someone to take this body out of here, before it starts stinkin' up the place.

(The body is taken away.)

PROF. *(Referring to body.)* Who could do such a thing?

(PROFESSOR looks at ESMIRELDA.)

ESMIRELDA. Well, it weren't me.

(PROFESSOR and ESMIRELDA look at TARA.)

TARA. Nor me. Violence, very vulgar.

(PROFESSOR, ESMIRELDA and TARA look at JOE.)

JOE. Baby, baby, baby.

(ALL gasp as they see the PERSON IN TRENCHCOAT who has reentered.)

PROF. *(Quiet.)* Who's that?
JOE. Some fool who doesn't realize it's 90 degrees outside.
TARA. That person frightens me.
ESMIRELDA. *(Loud.)* What do you want, you scoundrel?

(Pause as MAN IN TRENCHCOAT stares at them. Then he darts off.)

PROF. That was strange.
TARA. Indeed it was.
ESMIRELDA. That's what happens when you have prunes for breakfast.
PROF. Mrs. White.
ESMIRELDA. It is.

JOE. I haven't seen someone bolt so fast since the day Merv Griffin saw the construction of the Taj Mahal completed.

TARA. Well, I think we should put this tragedy behind us and move on to glories of Egypt's past. Let us all board "Nile Princess" for journey to place bucolic and treasure bountiful.

JOE. Well put, babe. I'm with you. But, before we board we should tell these folks what they're in for. Folks, there's been a murder, and you're going to help solve it and any other crimes which may occur. The dossiers you all received will help you, if you follow the "Rules of the Game": Remember. Do not open any of the seals on your dossier until instructed. And now, let us board the "Nile Princess".

(MUSIC in. Cast works the crowd. First course is served.)

Scene 2

(PROFESSOR takes front and center. ESMIRELDA exits. Music out.)

PROF. Ladies and gentlemen, may I have your attention please? The boat has just pulled away from the pier, and we are well on our way up the Nile. It has occurred to me that some of you have not paid for your passage. Would you kindly take care of that with Mrs. White. Where is Mrs. White? *(Calling.)* Mrs. White.

ESMIRELDA. *(Reenters.)* Danger, dangeer!

PROF. Mrs. White, cut out that nonsense and collect the

fares that are owed me.

ESMIRELDA. Yeah, yeah. From evenin' dusk to mornin' sun this maid's work is never done. Right,_____? *(Insert guest's name.)*

PROF. Put them in that envelope I gave you containing the other fares.

ESMIRELDA. Is that what was in that envelope?

PROF. Yes. Now do as I say.

ESMIRELDA. I gave the money away. I thought it was the tips for the boat crew.

PROF. Go get it back.

ESMIRELDA. The crew on the pier.

PROF. You are nothing but a mindless, careless, irresponsible bimbo!

ESMIRELDA. Oh, look what I found hidin' in me apron. It's the envelope of money.

PROF. I don't appreciate your sense of humor.

ESMIRELDA. Had y' goin' there for a while, didn't I?

PROF. I ought to throw you overboard.

ESMIRELDA. You better not do that, Professor, I can't swim.

PROF. (Evil.) Exactly. I think it's dinner time for the alligators.

ESMIRELDA. You're gonna have to catch me first.

PROF. Oh, I'll catch you.

(PROFESSOR chases ESMIRELDA, all the while she screams "Danger, Dangeeer." The chase ends as ESMIRELDA bumps into MICHAEL PETERS, who has just entered. ESMIRELDA is face to face with MICHAEL.)

ESMIRELDA. It's his ghost! Evil! There's evil on board.

MICHAEL. I'm not his ghost. I'm his twin brother, Michael Peters. Formerly with the F.B.I., now just a P. I. who's P. O.'d that his brother was D. O. A. just minutes ago.

TARA. How clever, a man who rhymes.

MICHAEL. Ea-sy, la-dy. Hey, where'd you get your dress? At a half-off sale?

JOE. Watch it, mister. That's my girl your shootin' remarks at.

MICHAEL. And it was my brother one of you mugs was shootin' bullets at. I want to know who it was, and I'm not leaving 'til I find him...

TARA. How do you know it was man?

MICHAEL. Or her. What's you name?

TARA. I am Princess Tara of Munchovnia.

MICHAEL. Munchovnia. Sounds like a Polish breakfast cereal.

PROF. *(To Michael.)* Hey, how did you get here so fast?

MICHAEL. I was next door in Libya gathering information for another client.

PROF. Who's your client?

MICHAEL. _____ *(Insert name of politician running for office.)* He wants to know Kadafi's strategy for staying in office.

JOE. Look, you're wasting your time here. The murderer was without a doubt this way-out dude in a trench coat. He fled the scene of the crime and never boarded the boat. So, you're in the wrong place.

MICHAEL. I don't think so. I have a letter here, a very suspicious letter found in my brother's coat pocket. It reads:

Dear Benjamin:

      I love you more than you know. If you don't reciprocate, I will take drastic measures.

Signed,

_____*(Guest.)*

Ms. _____, please stand, How long did you have these feelings for my brother? *(Answer.)* Does your husband know you were carrying on with my brother? *(Answer.)* What did you mean when you said you would take drastic measures if he did not reciprocate your love? *(Answer.)* Please sit. It seems you were not the only one who was romantically involved with my brother, Ms._____. A photo was found in his wallet, *(Big.)* A photo of Princess Tara!

TARA. Yes, I knew your brother... very intimately. We would rendezvous in Austrian Alps outside of Vienna, where we would sit by fire and sip cognac in our chalet.

MICHAEL, He's not the only one you were intimate with. I have an entire list of men. *(He unravels what seems to be an endless scroll of guests' names. He reads.)* Let's see. There was_____.

TARA. He was in Monaco.

MICHAEL. _____.

TARA. Paris.

MICHAEL. _____.

TARA. Copenhagen.

MICHAEL. Professor Dobson.

TARA. Him. He was cheap. He would take me to sleazy motel room in Amsterdam with mirrors on ceiling.

ESMIRELDA. He took you to that place, too?

PROF. Quiet, Mrs. White.

ESMIRELDA. I thought it was just the hired help he took to that place.

MICHAEL. I also understand that your relationship with

my brother did not end on positive terms.

TARA. I should say not.

MICHAEL. Kindly explain.

TARA. He became more interested in my extended family, than in me. So, I ended it.

MICHAEL. Did you also end his life?

TARA. I find your accusation unfounded, unfunny, uninteresting and totally uncouth.

MICHAEL. Yet, understandable.

TARA. What are you implying?

MICHAEL, Many of the men on this list have never lived to tell why you ended your relationship with them.

TARA. Joe, put this heathen in his place.

(JOE grabs MICHAEL by the shirt collar.)

JOE. Hey, Bub. You're hurtin' my girl's feelings. Now feelings are a real important thing. So lay off.

MICHAEL. That's a very interesting ring you have on your finger.

(JOE releases MICHAEL.)

JOE. I bought this one night after a non-stop winning streak at the crap table.

MICHAEL. It's a very rare design.

JOE. Yeah, well... I got taste.

MICHAEL. It's a rare Egyptian design. Tell me where you got the ring.

JOE. At a pawn shop in Vegas.

MICHAEL. *(Quick, strong.)* Where you really got the ring!

JOE. I told you.

MICHAEL. My brother had an identical ring. It was a family heirloom.

JOE. Bub, listen to me. If you think I'm lyin', you're knockin' on the wrong tree. If you think I stole this ring, you're barkin' up the wrong door; and, if you think you're lookin' at your brother's killer, clean the wax out of your ears.

MICHAEL. *(Strong.)* All of you listen to me. And listen good. My brother is dead, and I'm going to find the culprit responsible. Now, I want to know who was away from the scene of the crime at the time of the murder.

PROF. I was.

ESMIRELDA. I was.

JOE. I was.

TARA. I was.

(ZELDA LAVISH enters.)

ZELDA. And I was.

(ALL others gasp.)

ALL. Who... are... you?

ZELDA. Let the drums roll out, let the trumpets blow, strike up the band.

(ZELDA poses.)

ESMIRELDA. Strike up the band? Strike up the circus, seeing that the freak show just arrived.

ZELDA. Don't you all recognize me?

PROF. You're the chief of an Ethiopian bush tribe.

TARA. No, that is without a doubt Prince Charles in a dress.

JOE. No, no, no. I know. It's Ann Margaret... on steroids.

(ALL laugh.)

ZELDA. I'll have you know that I am Zelda lavish, world renowned art and antiquities dealer.

MICHAEL. Why are you here?

ZELDA. Why do you think?

ESMIRELDA. She wants to get her slippery hands on the treasure.

ZELDA. Who let the monkey out of its cage?

ESMIRELDA. Are you talkin' 'bout me?

ZELDA. I don't see any other beasts wandering about.

ESMIRELDA. Lady, what happened to your face? Some local tribe use you as a human sacrifice.

(ESMIRELDA laughs.)

ZELDA. *(With a flamboyant hand gesture.)* Sssss!

MICHAEL, Ladies please, this isn't helping anything.

JOE. No, but it's better than _____*(Insert popular primtime soap opera.)*

ZELDA. I say it's time to party. Waiter, I'll have a bottle of Dom Perignon with two glasses.

MICHAEL, Two glasses?

ZELDA. One for me; one for my escort.

MICHAEL. Your escort?

ZELDA. Yes, he dropped me off and said he'd return after midnight, after he had successfully destroyed Iraq's nuclear capability single-handedly.

MICHAEL. The only person capable of doing that is _____*(Guest.)* And he's right here

ZELDA. There's one other person. James Bond.

TARA. You know James Bond?

ZELDA. Me and 007 are like this.

(ZELDA clenches her fingers.)

TARA. Did he bring you here in his highly advanced air transport vehicle?

ZELDA. His new one. It travels at the speed of light. Just minutes ago, I was sipping cappucino in Venice.

JOE. I like Venice. I really dig the beaches... and those California babes. You know, that's where Princess Tara and I met.

TARA. She's not talking about that Venice.

JOE. Are you sure?

MICHAEL. So, you're here to view the treasure of King Pharclas.

ZELDA. I'm here to *obtain* the treasure of King Pharclas.

PROF. Impossible. The treasure belongs to me. You can pay to see it; you can pay more to touch it, and you can pay even more to have a photo taken with it. But you can't have it.

ZELDA. What's your price?

PROF. It's not for sale.

ZELDA. *(Pulls out a wad of money.)* Name your price.

JOE. Baby, I've got some great beach front property in Beirut you'd love. Talk t' me.

ZELDA. No.

JOE. How about a nuclear reactor at Chernobyl? It needs a few minor repairs, but...

MICHAEL. Get outta here. Do you always travel with that much money?

ZELDA. You never know what trinkets you'll want to purchase as souvenirs, as reminders of a good time had or an evil time avoided.

MICHAEL. Evil, huh?

ZELDA. Throughout history, one has always encountered evil where one has expected pleasure.

MICHAEL. There's been a murder, you know.

ZELDA. I know.

MICHAEL. What do you mean, you know?

PROF. What do you mean, you know?

ZELDA. James Bond received news of the calamity on his brainwaves.

MICHAEL. His brainwaves?

ZELDA. You know James, always a step a-*head* of his time?

(*Beat.*)

MICHAEL. Ladies and gentlemen, a coroner's report was expeditiously completed before I boarded the boat, and it states that my brother was taken down by a 22 calibre hand gun. *(To ZELDA, rapid dialogue.)* Do you own a gun?

ZELDA. Of course.

MICHAEL. Is it with you?

ZELDA. Of course.

MICHAEL. Is it a .22?

ZELDA. Of course.

MICHAEL. *(Big.)* Did you kill my brother?

ZELDA. Of course.

MICHAEL. *(Quick.)* Aha!

ZELDA. Not.

MICHAEL. Ms. Lavish, I'm going to keep my eye on you.

ZELDA. Not while I'm undressing, you'll see things you won't believe.

(Beat.)

MICHAEL. Ladies and gentlemen, I want to share something interesting with you. It's an ancient parchment found on my brother when he was taken to the hospital. The original message is written in hieratic script, a form of writing derived from Egyptian hieroglyphics. Next to this text is my brother's translation. It reads:

Dear Queen Mamria:

Despite the present conflict, I would like for you to have the treasure, which now rightfully be-longs to me.

Signed, King Kahtryes. *(Pronounced Káh-tree-us.)*
I don't know what significance this has, if any, but because it was on my brother at the time of his murder, I will consider it a clue, and I will bring it around to show all of you. Ladies and Gentlemen, the mystery web is quickly becoming entangled. I would like to inform you that there is one person and only one person in this room above suspicion: me. It is now time to open the first and only the first seal on your dossier. In addition to a limerick clue, you will find a piece of bribe money. Use this money to bribe your favorite suspect for a bit of information, which will help you solve the mystery. Each major suspect has only one bit of information to give, and you have but one bill to spend, so choose wisely. Because I am not a suspect I have no bribe clue to offer you. And now, let the bribing begin.

(MUSIC in. ALL work tables, being bribed. ESMIRELDA walks around with a bottle of vodka, which she depletes--getting progressively tipsy. MICHAEL shows the parchment clue. Entree is served.)

(GUESTS receive the Limerick Clue. When unscrambled, it reads:)

There is a person mysterious
Cunning, brazen and ingenious
Though seemingly droll
Possesses no soul
Than one evil and so devious

Duplicity is remembered well
'Twas easy then for greed to excel
The past is gone
The hate lives on
To the rival descendants, farewell

BRIBE CLUES

PROF. Look to the past to answer the questions of the present.

TARA. Diamonds are a girl's best friend, not murder.

JOE. You do what you have to do to make a buck.

ESMIRELDA. Loyalty is its own reward.

ZELDA. I deal in dusty antiquities, but my hands are clean.

Scene 3

(JOE takes the stage. ESMIRELDA, ZELDA and TARA are out. MICHAEL observes. MUSIC out.)

JOE. Ladies and Gentlemen, may I have your attention, please? Tonight is a very special night for me. It's my birthday. Now, I don't expect a lot of hoopla. After all, I am a modest kinda guy, but I would like to indulge just a wee bit and mark the occasion with a song. I selected one special, and I'd like to sing it for you. *(He sings.)*
Happy Birthday to me
Happy Birthday to me
Happy Birthday Dear Joe
Happy Birthday to me. *(He prompts applause for himself.)*
Gosh, I feel great. Thanks for sharin' that with me.

(ESMIRELDA staggers forward with an empty bottle of vodka in her hand. She is intoxicated.)

ESMIRELDA. Clear the way, Humpty Dumpty is here. *(To Guest.)* Hello, Humpty, so nice of you to come. Don't fall off your wall. *(To another.)* And there's Spencer Tracy. Spencer, how I love you and Katherine Hepburn. *(To another guest.)* Oh Diana, you came. I'm glad to see you're back with the Supremes. *(She does girl group movement.)*

JOE. Hey, babe, you all right?

ESMIRELDA. I'm perfectly fine. Nothing wrong with me. It's the darn bottle. Every time I gets me a full one, I turn me head and it's empty again.

JOE. Babe, alcohol is bad news.

ESMIRELDA. Your singing is bad news.

JOE. Why do you indulge?

ESMIRELDA. Because in a world of deceit, this stuff is truth.

JOE. Bottled truth, huh? I bet there's a market for that.

PROF. I'll go in on it with you. I'll run tours of the factory.

JOE. You're on. 80/20. I'm gonna make some calls.

(JOE exits.)

ESMIRELDA. There's a tempest brewing on board!

PROF. Esmirelda, sit down.

ESMIRELDA. You. You better beware. Evil will destroy you. Danger! There's danger on board!!

PROF. The only danger here is in your head, fool woman.

ESMIRELDA. Don't you go puttin' me down, or I'll spill everything I know.

PROF. Your bottle's empty. Go get another.

ESMIRELDA. You'd like that, wouldn't you? You'd like me to run out of here and let you continue rippin' off all these people.

PROF. I'm warning you, Esmirelda.

ESMIRELDA. Don't you warn me, you swindler.

PROF. That's enough.

ESMIRELDA. No, I'm not finished. See, folks, Dobson over there is takin' all your money so you can see a treasure that

don't exist. You're going to get to Aswam and they'll be nothin'
but a pile of glass gems and gold-painted chains. Some treasure.
(To PROFESSOR.) They oughta send you to the gallows, they
ought.

PROF. How dare you denigrate me in the presence of my
friends and colleagues.

ESMIRELDA. Your friends, your colleagues. Ha! They are
not friends. They are pawns in your sleazy profit-making hoax.
You're a bloody sham! But you'll get yours. *(Big.)* Evil always
begets evil!

(ESMIRELDA runs out laughing maniacally.)

PROF. Ladies and gentlemen, please excuse the inappro-
priate behavior of Mrs. White. Alcohol intoxication warps one's
sense of decorum and propriety. We'll be arriving in Aswan
very soon, and the *genuine* treasure of King Pharclas awaits
witness by you all. *(Pompous.)* It will be a glorious moment
when you, the first Westerners ever, lay eyes on it. Let me
recite a verse I wrote about the treasure. *(As he reads, his ex-
citement and verve wax, until he reaches a state of frenzy.)*

There is an Egyptian treasure
An ancient king's prize pleasure
It sparkles in light
A breathtaking sight
A fervent delight
Not one bit contrite
A bounty of might
My heart it exciiiites...

(Gunshots ring out, as he bellows his last word. He stumbles

and dies. ALL the suspects run to him, from different directions.)

MICHAEL. Well...
ALL. He's dead.

(As the body is carried away.)

ZELDA. Another one bites the dust.
TARA. He'll never take me to cheap motel again.
ESMIRELDA. Evil begets evil.
JOE. Maybe I can charge admission to his tombstone.
MICHAEL. Ladies and gentlemen, this senseless killing must stop. I will now be conducting my parade of suspects. This is an interrogation of my major suspects. After I am done with each of them, you will have the opportunity to ask questions. *(Opening up the interrogation to the guests is optional.)* Before I begin, I have noticed that written on the window in lipstick is the message: "I've waited centuries for this." Before I begin my questioning, let me read an excerpt from my brother's recent book entitled "A Kingdom of Treasures". This book focuses on the conflict between the ruling dynasties of Egypt. *(Reads.)*

Egypt has always been a land under siege. This desert nation's history was marked by frequent and intense power struggles between two rival empires: the Persian and the Assyrian.
What was most interesting about this dynastic conflict was that the ruling monarchs of each, King Kahtryes of Persia and Queen Mamria of Assyria, were romantically involved. Bloodshed filled their countrysides; passion filled their personal chambers.

King Kahtryes, pillaged the sacred temples of the Nile valley and looted their treasures. However, his indomitable love for Queen Mamria daunted his greed, and he gave all the treasures to his beloved. These treasures include jewels belonging to such pharoas as Ramses, Tut, and Pharclas. Kahtryes' giving the treasure to the Assyrian Queen so angered the Persian people that they massacred him, forced Queen Mamria into exile and declared an eternal war on Assyria, a country which later became called *Turkey.*

Very interesting. I believe this story will help me find the killer of my brother, for our family heritage is Turkish. I would first like to interrogate Joe Al-Abdul Dimici.

(JOE comes forward.)

JOE. Talk t'me.

MICHAEL. You are of Arab descent?

JOE. You got it. I'm Italian.

MICHAEL. Where did your relatives come from:

JOE. I got a couple of cousins in Newark. Some of them say we're related somehow to Frank Sinatra.

MICHAEL. Your *distant* relatives.

JOE. Well, I got a Aunt Concetta from Sicily who sweeps the sidewalks with her hair. And, I got an Uncle Omar from Baghdad who...

MICHAEL. You said Baghdad.

JOE. Yes, I did.

MICHAEL. Baghdad is in Iraq. Iraq was once part of Persia!

JOE. You're good with math.

MICHAEL. Tell me about your business dealings.

JOE. I am a man of many businesses. I got me this chain of Wee Willy Winkey Motels; I own the world's largest tea company, Teas-R-Us; and, I just started this wholesale jewel company which specializes in glass reproductions of famous gems called Glass Goodies.

MICHAEL. Where is this new business of your based?

JOE. Aswan.

MICHAEL. Aha!

JOE. No Aswan.

MICHAEL. *(Optional.)* Are there any questions for Mr. Dimici?

(Questions.)

MICHAEL. Next, Princess Tara of Munchovnia. *(She comes forward.)* Princess, I've had my eye on you.

TARA. Like all men, here, you've had *both* eyes on me.

MICHAEL. Especially the professor.

TARA. What you call men like him...

ESMIRELDA. Sleaze balls.

TARA. Yes.

MICHAEL. That surprise trip to that motel angered you.

TARA Disgusted me.

MICHAEL. You were also involved with my brother, weren't you?

TARA. Yes.

MICHAEL. Were you trying to get his treasure?

TARA. Treasure belong to Professor.

MICHAEL. He may have discovered it, but it rightfully belongs to the Turkish people. My brother was of Turkish descent.

ESMIRELDA. There is no treasure.

MICHAEL. There's a treasure all right. It's not the phoney one the Professor had replicated, but the *actual* treasure of King Pharclas.

ESMIRELDA. No one knows where that is.

MICHAEL. Wrong. My brother did. He knew its whereabouts. That's why he was here, to uncover and claim it.

TARA. Well, he didn't do very good job.

MICHAEL. Tell me something. Who founded Munchovnia?

TARA. My country has been ruled by many peoples: Ottomans, Persians, Roman, Egyptians... many peoples.

MICHAEL. One more question: what are you doing after this is over?

JOE. Nothin' with you, Bub.

MICHAEL. *(Optional.)* Are there any questions for Princess Tara.?

(Questions.)

MICHAEL, Next, Esmirelda White. *(She comes forward.)* You've been warning us of danger ever since we assembled.

ESMIRELDA. I was right. Wasn't I?

MICHAEL. I'm afraid that you were. I wonder if you were also responsible.

ESMIRELDA. Oh, gobildy gook.

MICHAEL. I have in my possession an unmailed letter from you to Professor Dobson. It was found in your Cairo flat and faxed to me. It reads:

Dear Professor, If you do not give me a raise, spelled r.a.z.e., I will make you pay the consequences.

Why the threat?

ESMIRELDA. You know, I come from a line of proud people.

If we do not get what we feel we deserve, we take action.

MICHAEL. Such as murder.

ESMIRELDA. Mr. Peters, let me tell you something my Auntie Martha used to say: The early bird catches the worm, but the bird that sticks around gets the rat.

MICHAEL. You're still here.

ESMIRELDA. I am.

MICHAEL. Did you get the rat?

ESMIRELDA. I'll never tell.

MICHAEL. *(Optional.)* Any questions for Mrs. White?

(Questions.)

MICHAEL. Finally, I would like to question Zelda Lavish. *(She comes forward.)* I cannot figure you out.

ZELDA. There are men of science who cannot figure me out.

MICHAEL. What is your family heritage?

ZELDA. Part French, Part Middle Easter, part...

MICHAEL. Middle Eastern?

ZELDA. Yes.

MICHAEL. You deal in art and antiquities, and you came on this cruise to purchase the treasure of King Pharclas. Right?

ZELDA. Correct.

MICHAEL. You plans must have changed now that the treasure we're sailing toward is phoney.

ZELDA. That treasure is as real as you want it to be. Everything is an illusion.

MICHAEL. Is that what you tell your clients?

ZELDA. That's what I tell my husband.

MICHAEL. *(Surprised.)* Your husband?

ZELDA. Well, fiancé. We never did get the chance to tie the knot.

MICHAEL. Tie the knot withwhom?

(Pause.)

ZELDA. You brother!

MICHAEL. *(Flabbergasted.)* You mean, my brother and... and ... you!

ZELDA. And why not?! After being hooked up with thunder cleavage over there, it was time he had a real lady.

TARA. Then why did he pick you?

ZELDA. Darlin', why don't you step outside? There's a Mac truck missing it's headlights.

TARA. You know, Ms. Lavish... *(Rapid dialogue.) You* are annoying.

ZELDA. *You* are aggravating.

TARA. *You* are irritating.

ZELDA. *You* are cunning.

TARA. *(With suspicion.) You* are interesting.

ZELDA. *You* are *not!*

(Pause.)

MICHAEL. Ms. Lavish, what is it that you're hiding?

ZELDA. Whatever it is, it is well-hidden.

(ZELDA starts to exit.)

MICHAEL. Hey, where are you going?

ZELDA. I'm leaving to get my beauty rest.

TARA. Don't set the alarm.

ZALDA. Ssss!

MICHAEL. Get back here.

ZELDA. What is it?

MICHAEL. *(Optional.)* Questions. Are there any questions for Zelda? *(Questions. After several...)* I have one more question for you.

ZELDA. Well, get on with it. This is such a drag!

(ZELDA reacts.)

MICHAEL. How tall are you?

ZELDA. 6' 3".

MICHAEL. Is that with heels?

ZELDA. With anyone.

MICHAEL. Ladies and gentlemen, I now know who the killer is. I'll need a few moments to organize my facts, and then I shall have a resolution for you. You, too, can offer your solutions. Please open the final seal on your dossiers. You will find a Murder a la Carte Resolution Form. Expeditiously fill it in, listing the murderer or murderers, the motives, the weapons used and any accomplices. Your forms will be collected shortly. Truth will come to light. Justice will triumph. Good luck.

Scene 4

(JOE takes center stage.)

JOE. Folks, can I have your attention please. I just want to say I'm really enjoying being with all of you here aboard the

"Nile Princess". You evoke a warmth like the audiences who used to cheer me on during my days as a singer. Yes, before my days as a handsome, wealthy dude, I was a handsome, musical dude--a headliner in Atlantic City. Sure I was. You could catch my show, three o'clock every Tuesday morning in the downstairs lounge of Billy's Lonestar Bar, Grill and Casino. I packed 'em in. But I'm said to say that when opportunity knocked, and I had the chance to open a chain of Wee Willy Winkey Motels, I closed the cover on the black and white and chased the green. I'll never forget those days, though--those days when I'd look out and see an audience, a real live audience smashing chairs over each other's heads. What a feelin'. You know, in those days I warmed the heart of many a gorgeous babe with my golden voice. But none so gorgeous as_____ *(Guest)*. _____, come on up here. I've got something special I want to sing to you.

(Guest joins JOE. He sings a "lounge lizard" song, inserting the following patter.)

JOE. You know,_____, feelings are important. They make us who we are. If we don't feel, we don't exist. How are you feelin'? Good? *(Answer.)* Good. *(JOE finishes the song. Guest sits.)* Thank you. Thank you all very much.

(MICHAEL takes front and center.)

(NOTE: Dialogue and stage direction from the beginning of Scene 4 to this point, are optional.)

RESOLUTION

MICHAEL. Ladies and Gentlemen, after two grisly murders, those of my brother, Benjamin Peters, and Professor Dillon Dobson, I now know who the murderer is. Yes, one person is responsible for these two heinous deeds. Let's look at the evidence. We have a limerick which... *(Reads.)*

Tells of a person mysterious

Cunning, brazen and ingenious

Though seemingly droll

Possesses no soul

Than one evil and so devious

Our killer was cunning and devious! A person who ingeniously masqueraded in front of all us as just another passenger on our cruise up the Nile. *(Beat, Strong.)* "Beware the guise!" our first victim warned us. But we did not heed his call. As a famous writer once said: "Murder and intrigue the Nile doth breed!". Well, the murder has ended, but the intrigue is just beginning, as I uncover the motive for these dastardly crimes. The writing was on the wall, or should I say the window. *(Very strong.)* "I've waited centuries for this!" Centuries for revenge. Revenge for what?! Lets find our culprit. Mr. Dimici.

JOE. Talk t'me.

MICHAEL. You intrigue me.

JOE. You marvel me.

MICHAEL. You openly admitted that you are of Arab descent.

JOE. Don't forget the Italian part, you'll upset dear Pop.

MICHAEL. Our killer is an Arab descendant and is here seeking revenge for the plundering of his homeland centuries ago.

JOE. Did I ever tell you, you have great resonance in your voice? You should be behind a microphone.

MICHAEL. As my brother's book said, "Egypt has always been a country under siege." You are continuing this siege, in your own greedy way, with the manufacturing of glass rip offs of Egypt's treasures.

JOE. A little Western capital for a country ravaged by Depression.

MICHAEL. Was there also a capital offense involved?

JOE. Hey, Mister. If you think you're lookin' at a killer, you're tryin' to fit a round peg into a bread box.

MICHAEL. You were away from the scene of the crime both times.

JOE. Purely circumstantial evidence.

MICHAEL. Anyone who sings "Happy Birthday" to himself has to be guilty of something.

JOE. Call me vain, if you like, but don't call me a murderer.

TARA. Mr. Peters, Joe may be egotistical, greedy, selfish pain-in-the-neck, but he couldn't hurt a fly.

MICHAEL. You're right. He couldn't. You're not our killer, Mr. Dimici. You're too much of a wimp.

JOE. Ladies and gentlemen, now that my good name has been cleared, I'm lending it to a super new product due out on the market next year. It's the Dimici Doll. It's a miniature replica of me in a god lamé suit, holding a microphone. You push a little button on my back, and I sing Elvis Presley tunes. Our slogan is: "The King lives in Dimici". Catchy, huh? If you want a piece of the action, you'll have to contact my prime investor,_____(Guest)

MICHAEL. Ladies and Gentlemen, let's look at more of the evidence. We have a second limerick which reads: *(Reads.)*

Duplicity is remembered well

'Twas easy then for greed to excel

The past is gone

The hate lives on

To the descendants, farewell.

We know here that *greed* is the key to this mystery, the greed of the Turks centuries ago. This, too, was established in my brother's book. *(Reads.)*

"King Kahtryes, leader of Persia, pillaged the sacred temples of the Nile valley and looted their treasures."

Then, he gave the treasure to the Assyrian or the *Turkish* Queen. This angered the Turks so, that they waged "An eternal war" on Persia, a war which continues today. It seems, then, that our Arab killer, would be Persian. Who here is greedy? Who here is Persian? Princess Tara is.

TARA. I am not Persian. I am Munchovnian.

MICHAEL. You told us yourself that your country was ruled by many peoples: Ottomans, Egyptians, Romans, *Persians.*

TARA. That was centuries ago.

MICHAEL. Exactly. You wanted the treasure. My brother knew where it was.

TARA. And now he is dead.

MICHAEL. He was of Turkish descent--a prime target for a Persian murderer.

TARA. I am not Persian.

MICHAEL. What about Professor Dobson?

TARA. Sleaze ball.

MICHAEL. He may not have had the treasure, but he was blaspheming it by running tours to a phoney replica of it. A

Persian would certainly want him out of the picture.

TARA. I am not Persian.

MICHAEL. And then there's your late arrival. I know may Persians. They're always late.

TARA. I am not Persian!

MICHAEL. There's one and only one reason why you could have killed our victims.

TARA. What is that?

MICHAEL. You're *not* Persian.

TARA. I am confused.

MICHAEL. Our murderer was not Persian.

TARA. I am very confused.

MICHAEL. Our murderer was Egyptian!

TARA. I think perhaps you should call in Columbo for some assistance.

MICHAEL. *(Excited.)* No, I have a firm grip on this one. See... our killer had nothing to do with the "eternal war" waged on the Turks. Our killer was here avenging a duplicitous act, which was committed hundreds of years before that. That act was the *initial* pillaging of her ancestors' treasure. Our killer is obviously...

ZELDA. Don't even say it! I could have killed those two morons. Neither of them would take me to the treasure before you beasts got there, so that I could examine it, and neither of them would sell it to me, which was why I came to Egypt.

MICHAEL. Yes.

ZELDA. I could have gotten a pretty penny for that treasure.

MICHAEL. Yes.

ZELDA. And I had motive to kill...

MICHAEL. Yes.

ZELDA. And I have a .22...

MICHAEL. Yes.

ZELDA. And I'm Egyptian.

MICHAEL. No.

ZELDA. What do you mean, no?

MICHAEL. You're not Egyptian.

ZELDA. How dare you...

MICHAEL. You're not even Zelda Lavish.

ZELDA. Of course I am.

MICHAEL. No, you're not. You're the weirdo in the trenchcoat. You're Melvin Lavinsky: An unemployed antiques dealer from Hoboken, New Jersey, who came here hoping to get her hands on the treasure for her daughter.

ZELDA. *(Rips off wig, Speaks with a deep Jewish accent.)* Yeah, yeah. You got me. I'm Melvin Lavinsky, a modest business man from New Jersey who wanted to give something special to his daughter, Sookie, for her Bas Mitzvah. I didn't want the whole treasure, just a trinket or two. And I surely didn't kill no one. You gotta believe me.

MICHAEL. I believe you.

ZELDA. Thank you. Folks, if you're ever in Hoboken, stop in to my little shop, and I'll give a ten percent discount. *(ZELDA'S voice.)* Unless you're _____*(Guest)*, then you have to pay full price.

MICHAEL. Ladies and gentlemen, our killer is an Egyptian descendant. She came here to protect her family treasure. She let neither my brother, nor Professor Dobson stand in her way. She is the great, great, great, great, great, great, great, great granddaughter of King Pharclas. Esmirelda White!

(ESMIRELDA enters looking stunning. She speaks with so-phistication.)

ESMIRELDA. Yes, I killed them. I killed them both. The professor was making a mockery of my family name with his greed. And your brother was trying to get a treasure, which rightfully belongs to me. *(Cockney.)* But I fooled all of you. Ha, ha, ha. And *(Regular voice.)* I got my revenge. *(Big.)* Loyalty is its own reward! *(Pulls gun.)* Now, out of my way. I'm off to get *my* treasure.

(ZELDA pulls a gun and shoots ESMIRELDA.)

ZELDA. *(Zelda's voice.)* That's for killing two innocent people. *(Shoots again.)* That's for ruining my chance to get the treasure *(Shoots again.)* And, that's for the tacky dress.

(ESMIRELDA falls dead.)

MICHAEL. There you have it, ladies and gentlemen, Murder a la Carte's *Death and Deceit on the Nile.*

(BOWS. AWARDS.)

END OF PLAY

CLUES

1. Limerick Clue (Dossier)
> There is a person mysterious
> Cunning, brazen and ingenious
> Though seemingly droll
> Possesses no soul
> Than one evil and so devious
>
> Duplicity is remembered well
> 'Twas easy then for greed to excel
> The past is gone
> The hate lives on
> To the rival descendants, farewell

2. Lipstick Clue (Mirror.)
> I've waited centuries for this.

3. Parchment Clue
> Page 24.

4. Book Clue
> Page 29

5. Bribe Clue
> Loyalty is its own reward

OTHER TITLES AVAILABLE FROM SAMUEL FRENCH

ELECTION DAY
Josh Tobiessen

Full Length / Comedy / 2m, 2f / Unit Set

It's Election Day, and Adam knows his over-zealous girlfriend will never forgive him if he fails to vote. But when his sex starved sister, an eco-terrorist, and a mayoral candidate willing to do anything for a vote all show up, Adam finds that making that quick trip to the polls might be harder than he thought. *Election Day* is a hilarious dark comedy about the price of political (and personal) campaigns.

"An outrageous comedy… at double-espresso speed."
- *The New York Times*

"Ridiculously entertaining… cute and cutting."
- *Variety*

"Laugh-out-loud."
- *Backstage*

"Delightfully farcical… Tobiessen takes a simple premise and spins it out into a hilarious sequence of events. His dialogue is lean and playful, and includes some terrific lines."
- *Theatermania*

OTHER TITLES AVAILABLE FROM SAMUEL FRENCH

BACH AT LEIPZIG
Itamar Moses

Comedy Farce / 7m / Interior

Leipzig, Germany — 1722. Johann Kuhnau, revered organist of the Thomaskirche, suddenly dies, leaving his post vacant. The town council invites musicians from across to audition for the coveted position, among them young Johann Sebastian Bach. In an age where musicians depend on patronage from the nobility or the church to pursue their craft, the post at a prominent church in a cultured city is a near guarantee of fame and fortune – which is why some of the candidates are willing to resort to any lengths to secure it. *Bach at Leipzig* is a fugue-like farcical web of bribery, blackmail, and betrayal set against the backdrop of Enlightenment questions about humanity, God, and art.

OTHER TITLES AVAILABLE FROM SAMUEL FRENCH

DEAD CITY
Sheila Callaghan

Full Length / Comic Drama / 3m, 4f / Unit Set

It's June 16, 2004. Samantha Blossom, a chipper woman in her 40s, wakes up one June morning in her Upper East Side apartment to find her life being narrated over the airwaves of public radio. She discovers in the mail an envelope addressed to her husband from his lover, which spins her raw and untethered into an odyssey through the city... a day full of chance encounters, coincidences, a quick love affair, and a fixation on the mysterious Jewel Jupiter. Jewel, the young but damaged poet genius, eventually takes a shine to Samantha and brings her on a midnight tour of the meat-packing district which changes Samantha's life forever—or doesn't. This 90 minute comic drama is a modernized, gender-reversed, relocated, hyper-theatrical riff on the novel Ulysses, occurring exactly 100 years to the day after Joyce's jaunt through Dublin.

"Wonderful... Sheila Callaghan's pleasingly witty and theatrical new drama that is a love letter to New York masquerading as hate mail... [Callaghan] writes with a world-weary tone and has a poet's gift for economical description.
The entire dead city comes alive..."
- *New York Times*

"*Dead City*, Sheila Callaghan's riff on James Joyce's Ulysses is stylish, lyrical, fascinating, occasionally irritating, and eminently worthwhile... the kind of work that is thoroughly invigorating."
- *Backstage*

OTHER TITLES AVAILABLE FROM SAMUEL FRENCH

JACK GOES BOATING
Bob Glaudini

Full Length / Comedy / 2m, 2f / Interior

Four flawed but likeable lower-middle-class New Yorkers interact in a touching and warmhearted play about learning how to stay afloat in the deep water of day-to-day living. Laced with cooking classes, swimming lessons and a smorgasbord of illegal drugs, *Jack Goes Boating* is a story of date panic, marital meltdown, betrayal, and the prevailing grace of the human spirit.

"An immensely likable play [that] exudes a wry compassion."
- The New York Times

"Endearing romantic comedy about a married couple and the social-misfit friends they fix up. Witty and knowing and all heart."
- Variety

"Glides effortlessly from the shallow end of the emotional pool to the deep end."
- Theatremania.com

OTHER TITLES AVAILABLE FROM SAMUEL FRENCH

JUMP/CUT
Neena Beber

Full Length / Drama / 2m, 1f /

Three bright urbanites want to make their mark on the world. Paul, a master of irony and distance, is a hardworking film maker on the rise. His girlfriend Karen, a grad student, must get on with her thesis or find a life outside of academia. Dave, a life long buddy whose brilliance is being consumed by increasingly severe episodes of manic depression, is camping on Paul's couch. Paul and Karen decide to turn Paul into a documentary. The camera is on 24 hours a day, capturing up close images of his jags and torpors and their responses. How far will love, friendship and ambition take this hip trio?

"Could not be more timely...
Fearlessly dives into provocative issues and ideas."
- Washington Times

"Savvy, solid play... about our fascination with victims and voyeurism, ...friendship and ambition, striving and its worth. Beber builds her characters... carefully with efficient and graceful layers of personalities and ideas... An accomplished piece of work structurally sound, snappily written and shot though with humor."
- Washington City Paper

"A sharp, funny, heartbreaking play that just pulls you in."
- Montgomery Community Television

"Quick and sharp... [with] something to say about the emotional environment we live in." *-The Georgetowner*

"A remarkable, absorbing, complex and intelligent play." *-Variety*

Winner of the L. Arnold Weissberger Award